Subversive Orthodoxy

Traditional Faith and
Radical Commitment

Kenneth Leech

Anglican Book Centre
Toronto, Ontario

1992
Anglican Book Centre
600 Jarvis Street
Toronto, Ontario
Canada M4Y 2J6

Typesetting by Jay Tee Graphics Ltd.

Canadian Cataloguing in Publication Data

Leech, Kenneth
  Subversive orthodoxy: traditional faith and
radical commitment

Based on 3 lectures delivered at the Trinity
Divinity associates' annual conference, Trinity
College, Toronto in May 1991.
ISBN 0-921846-49-5

1. Church renewal. I. Title.

BV600.2.L44 1992   362'.001'7   C92-093419-6

Contents

Preface *5*

1 The Birth of a Monster:
Racism and Christian Identity *7*

2 Comfort or Transformation?:
the Crisis of Modern Spirituality *30*

3 The Future:
towards a Subversive Orthodoxy *44*

References *59*

Preface

This book contains the lectures which I delivered to the Divinity Associates of Trinity College, Toronto, at their Annual Conference in May 1991. I am grateful to the Associates for permission to reprint them. In order not to delay publication, and because I want the book to be a basis for further discussion and debate and not an authoritative utterance, I have reprinted the lectures almost exactly as they were delivered. I would hope at some future date to develop many of the ideas contained in them at greater length.

Kenneth Leech

Feast of the Assumption,
15th August 1991.

1

The Birth of a Monster: Racism and Christian Identity

In 1958 a series of violent disturbances occurred in the streets around St Clement's Church in the Notting Dale district of London. They became known, rather inaccurately, as the "Notting Hill race riots," and were the first significant post-war attacks on Britain's small but growing black community. The riots were not major events but they were historically important for two reasons. First, the judge who sentenced those responsible for the violence described them as a small and insignificant section of the population—a view of racism which was to prevail for many years. Racism, on this view, was the work of a regrettable deviant minority within a tolerant community. Secondly, the incidents led within twenty-four hours to calls not for increased resistance to prejudice and discrimination but for control of immigration.

Thus were laid the foundations for the birth of a monster: the monster of racially based legislation and the reinforcement of prejudice and hatred. Thus was born, in the memorable words of the late Ruth Glass, "a new doctrine of original sin combined with a new faulty political arithmetic."[1] There was a third aspect of the disturbances which is of importance to the Christian community: the churches by and large were as unresponsive to the outbreaks of racial violence as they had been to the arrival of the immigrants themselves. It was in these years that the movement of black Christians away from the mainstream churches, particularly from the Church of England, began.

That year is of particular importance to me, for it was then, a few weeks after the riots, that I arrived in London as a student. I moved into the East End, and it is here that the bulk of my ministry, and of my adult life, has been spent. I arrived in London as the tension aroused by the Notting Dale events was still in the air. As the Lambeth Conference was meeting nearby, the atmosphere in inner London was tense; swastikas and "Keep Britain White" slogans were appearing on the walls.

I begin in a very personal way, by locating my theological perspective within the context of my own ministry in East London, and specifically within the context of urban racial inequality and oppression. I want to use the experience of racism as a lens through which to examine the nature of, the distortions of, and the prospects for, the Christian community. I will reflect (in Chapter Two) on the contemporary resurgence of interest in "spirituality" and, in critiquing this concept, will suggest that the idea of spirituality as an independent area of activity, somehow different from Christian existence and from the Christian community, is fraught with great danger. And, thirdly, I will raise some questions about the nature of orthodoxy, of tradition, and of Catholicity.

Because such an enterprise carries with it the danger of vagueness and of painting on an impossibly broad canvas, I will root each chapter within the ground of one specific tradition, a tradition which carries with it its strengths and weaknesses, its vision and its pathology, its potential for change and the real possibility of exhaustion, collapse, and extinction: the tradition known as Anglo-Catholicism. But I want to do this not in an elitist, narrow, or introverted way, but as a way of focussing and of relating the concrete and the specific to wider issues in the Christian world.

I would want, before I close the book, to have raised the question of whether we are for ever to be imprisoned within the false polarities of "liberal" and "conservative," "trendy" and "traditionalist," words which, in their current use, have become almost meaningless, and a way of closing discussion; or whether there is a dynamic, liberating, orthodoxy within which we can find both roots and impetus for change. My own position will become clearer if I say that the influences on my approach to Christianity are people like Thomas Merton, William Stringfellow, Dorothy Day, Conrad Noel, Michael Ramsey, and Trevor Huddleston; and, at the present time, Rowan Williams, Beverly Harrison, and Cornel West.

Let me begin with some personal history which has itself occurred within the wider social and political history of the East End. It is a history which focusses upon two streets, Cable Street and Brick Lane.[2] Cable Street was my home from 1958 until 1963; Brick Lane has been the main thoroughfare of the neighbourhood where I have worked, with interruptions, for the past sixteen years. Together they form a microcosm of the history both of East London and of urban social processes in many western cities.

Cable Street, as it was in the 1950s and 60s, was the classic urban slum, a combination of skid row and urban ghetto. Here, in property condemned as unfit for human habitation before World War One, had grown up a dockland café society, the social centre for merchant seamen from many parts of the world, as well as a place of refuge for the homeless and the despairing, the main London centre for young prostitutes, and the home of what, in contemporary sociological jargon, would be termed an "underclass." "It is the filthiest, dirtiest, most repellently odoured street in Christendom," wrote one author in 1961,[3] while a few years earlier a black American writer had contrasted it unfavourably with the "good-natured exuberance" of Harlem. In contrast, he said, the atmosphere of Cable Street was mysterious, sinister, and violent.[4] But perhaps the most perceptive account was by Patrick O'Donovan in a broadcast on BBC Radio in February 1950 on "The Challenge of Cable Street." O'Donovan described "a sense of hopelessness and of poverty that has ceased to struggle." He was horrified by the stretch of the street which was later to become my home. "I think these few hundred yards are about the most terrible in London."[5]

Cable Street was my first introduction to the urban experience of racism. Not that the neighbourhood itself was marked by inter-racial conflicts; on the contrary, it was one part of the East End where a variety of racial groups mixed freely. But the neighbourhood, "the coloured quarter" as it was known,[6] was effectively isolated from the rest of London. In the growth of this and other racial enclaves, we saw the beginnings of a "politics of race and residence" which was to shape the future of London's black communities and the shape of racial inequality in all British cities.[7]

The history of Brick Lane is quite different. A very long East End street, joining Whitechapel to Shoreditch, Brick Lane once stood at the centre of a community of Huguenot silk weavers who had fled from persecution in Europe. By the end of the nineteenth century it had become the heart of the Jewish ghetto, the new home for refugees from Russia and Poland after the assassination of the Tsar in 1881. By the mid 1970s the Jews had been replaced by Bengalis as the largest Bengali community in the world outside of Bangladesh itself grew up here. The old Huguenot church at the corner of Fournier Street and Brick Lane, which had become a synagogue in the nineteenth century, become a mosque in the twentieth. For most of the new arrivals, Muslim individuals and families from three villages in rural Sylhet, the streets of London were cold and unwelcoming. By the mid 1960s, before Bangladesh existed as a separate nation, observers were noticing a growing hostility against "Pakistanis"—an umbrella term used abusively to describe anyone from the sub-continent—and in 1969 the phenomenon of "Paki-bashing" grew up among the new skinhead gangs on the Collingwood Estate in nearby Bethnal Green.

Yet, unlike Cable Street, where the atmosphere was one of despair and an experience of neglect resulting in a kind of social autism, the climate in Brick Lane was marked by a determination that the community would not be defeated by racist violence. Like the Jewish radicals of an earlier era, the new Bengali immigrants began to organise, to resist, and to create their own religious, cultural, and political structures.

As Cable Street was my home in the 50s and 60s, so Brick Lane was to be my home and workplace in the late 70s, 80s, and 90s. It has been here, in this district with its rich cultural history, that my theology, politics, and reflection have been worked out.

As I reflect on the place of these two old London streets, both in my spiritual journey and in the corporate memory of the East End, I see and hear so many of the movements, upheavals, crises, and changes which have gone to make up the recent history of many cities. There is the centuries-old gulf between rich and poor, the gulf which led to the "outcast London" of the Victorian age. There is the residential segregation of poor people, often reinforced by, and itself reinforcing, racial inequality. There is the long-established phenomenon of population decline in the inner urban areas, leading to the collapse of the manufacturing base of many cities and the fragmentation of local community. There is the alarming and often fatal division between rich and poor neighbourhoods, evident in such issues as health care, with districts such as ours showing very high rates of respiratory disease, perinatal mortality, schizophrenia, and illnesses relating to housing damp. And there has been, since the 1960s, the phenomenon of "gentrification," a term coined by Ruth Glass towards the end of the 1950s to describe the process by which ghettoes of the wealthy and of the intelligentsia serve to intensify the pressure on space, and accelerate the squeezing out of poor people from many central city districts.[8]

I see and hear also many of the movements, upheavals, crises, and changes which affect churches all over the western world: churches which, finding themselves left behind in changing neighbourhoods, sometimes become introverted cultic shrines, bastions of an esoteric religious culture against the oncoming tides of immigrants, ritual re-enactments of the old order in districts of transition. Here, fearful and perplexed at the speed of change, church congregations have at times become a new type of Herbert Gans's "urban villagers," clinging together for warmth and fellowship, while outside the cruel winds usher in a climate which they cannot understand, skies whose formation they cannot discern.

It was in the Brick Lane district in the early 1970s that there occurred a development which was to disfigure the face of my parish and poison its atmosphere for over a decade, the revival, after some years of decay and marginalisation, of Neo-Nazism. It was in the Bethnal Green and Shoreditch parts of East London that Sir Oswald Mosley had built up the fascist movement in the 1930s, exploiting the resentments and fears of the urban villages adjacent to large refugee Jewish communities from both Eastern and Central Europe. In 1967, the National Front, a new fascist party, was formed out of three earlier movements, and by 1973 it had established its principal London stronghold in the streets around St Matthew's Church in Bethnal Green. Week by week, its supporters would gather in the streets by the church to sell their inflammatory newspapers. They created a climate of racial hatred and fear which contributed to, if it did not create, the growth of racial violence and harassment in the neighbourhood. 1978 was the peak year for racially motivated killings, and also for the radicalisation of the Muslim youth as they saw their homes and communities besieged. It was a year of decision too for many Christian people. Were they to retreat into their ecclesiastical ghettoes, to pray, to lament the violence, and to wait for better days? Or was there a prophetic testimony against evil, a call to resistance and solidarity, which would lead them into the streets alongside their Asian comrades? It was at heart an old dilemma, an old division between two conflicting understandings of the nature of the Christian community: one an inward, spiritual, and essentially sectarian view, the other a more historically located, dynamic view of a community forever in movement and forever under judgment.

Let me now go back some years to the late 1950s. When I arrived in the East End, I was aware that I was entering into a place where a vigorous movement of radical Christian witness had grown up in the 1870s and was still present: a tradition which I will call "subversive orthodoxy." Subversive because those Christians who were part of this movement were nonconformists, people at odds with and in conflict with prevailing injustice, people who were passionate in their advocacy for the poor and the dispossessed. Yet orthodox because it was their sense of the contradiction between the faith they professed and the conditions they encountered which was the driving force of their witness. This tradition had grown up when the sacramental religion of the Oxford Movement encountered the Christian socialism of the heirs of F. D. Maurice, an encounter which took place in a unique and unparalleled way in the East End. Within a few weeks of my arrival I was to meet three East End pastors who stood within this tradition and whose ministries were to have a permanent effect on my life.

Brother Neville Palmer was a shy Franciscan priest, born in Prince Edward Island, who had, in 1944, been sent by his community to begin a work of prayer and service in the Cable Street district. Taking over one of the many brothels, the Franciscans converted it into a "house of hospitality" on Catholic Worker lines. Neville was a major influence on my life. More than anyone else he taught me to pray, by example rather than method, and to see the integral unity of prayer and action, contemplation and social struggle. From him I began to understand the earthiness of doctrine, and of the doctrine of incarnation in particular; to see that doctrine was tested and tried, purified and realised, in concrete witness, life, and conflict. Neville lived out the incarnational theology, the truth of the Word made flesh, in the concrete reality of Cable Street. From him I began to learn that the servant church must be a prayerful church; that the pursuit of justice must go hand in hand with the deepening of love and humility; that the struggle for racial equality had to begin with the creation of more just and equal relations at the local level; and that the church, located at the heart of a situation of conflict, must be a silent, listening community before it became a community of discourse.

A hundred yards away from the Franciscan house was the flamboyant, charismatic figure of Father Joe Williamson, who compaigned for the demolition of the slum property and pioneered pastoral ministry with prostitutes all over Britain. Father Joe was the last of the ritualist slum priests of the Dolling tradition. He pushed that tradition—clerical, paternalist, and individualist—to its farthermost limits, and, in so doing, inadvertently helped to prepare the way for a new model of priesthood. He was first and foremost a pastor, and his life was devoted to the care and defence of the neglected and the downtrodden. An old-fashioned Anglo-Catholic, with a preaching style more akin to the Salvation Army, he believed that it was the world—and specifically the streets and homes of Whitechapel—which was the context of the church's ministry. He saw the church not as a sanctuary to be protected against contamination, but as a resource centre from which he and others were sent forth into the mess and danger of the battle.

The third of these radical East End priests who helped to share my theology and ministry was Stanley Evans. Of the three, he was the most disturbing, the most prophetic, and the most visionary. Evans was a pioneer of the parish communion movement as long ago as the mid-1950s, and he saw the church, not as an end in itself, but as a herald of God's

Kingdom. He believed that the church's social and political witness began with the raising of consciences and consciousness of the local Christian community, and therefore saw theology as a vital component of the church in the back streets. In the 1950s Evans was emphasizing that the most fundamental division between Christians was not a division running along denominational or confessional lines: it was, he argued, a division between those Christians in all churches who believed, in some sense, in the coming of God's Kingdom on earth, and those who did not. In his little parish in the back streets of East London, Evans anticipated much that was later to appear as liberation theology, though that term was not used until three years after his death.

Because my encounters with these priests and their ministries took place within the framework of racism and of the struggle for racial justice, I began to look at the parish itself in terms of its prophetic, critical, and conflictual role, as a social force for righteousness in the district. The very use of the terms "parish" and "district" to describe different realities raises important questions, for *paroikia* (Greek) and *parochia* (Latin) both mean "district," and when Theodore of Tarsus in the seventh century created the parish system in Britain, he was building on pre-Christian land arrangements. The whole notion of a parish is rooted in geography. The community of faith which meets for worship and witness does so within, and related to, a specific context. In our case, in Bethnal Green in the 1970s, that context was also the context of racist organising and racist faith.

The churches of the 1950s, confronted by numbers of immigrants from the Caribbean, including Barbados, the most Anglican country in the world, failed to respond: the stories of rejection, coldness, embarrassment, and lack of welcome are painful and all too numerous. By the time the church awoke to the challenge presented by racial discrimination and oppression to the claims of Christian faith, a generation of black Christians had been lost to the church.

The churches of the 1970s and 1980s were faced with a different challenge: that of racial violence and hatred, addressed mainly to Asian people, of non-Christian backgrounds. It was a challenge, not to love and accept the believer from another culture, but to defend the dignity and rights of a community under attack, a challenge to the very nature of humanity itself.

At its heart the question before us was: Is the parish, this primary fabric of Christian consciousness, a structure which exists only for its own membership, or does it witness to truths and values which must be proclaimed within, and over and against, the surrounding culture? Does the church serve the Kingdom? And, confronted by the alternative gospel of racism, does the church address the public arena?

The shape and form of British racism was changing very dramatically during these years. In broad terms there were three phases, each of them related to movements of immigration and to the ideology and legislation developed to respond to, and control, these movements.

First, there was a kind of laissez-faire period from the end of World War Two to 1962, during which cheap labour was encouraged and recruited from the West Indies. But those who were most needed on the labour market found that they were not wanted on the housing market. For "it was their labour that was wanted, not their presence."[9] The immediate response to the Notting Dale disturbances of 1958 was a demand for control. Without such control, argued Cyril Osborne, MP for Louth in the 1950s and 60s, "England will be handed over to a majority of coloured immigrants and the English race doomed to destruction."[10] By June 1961 the Home Secretary, R.A. Butler, assured the country: "If you give the Government a little longer, we shall try to find a solution as friendly to these people as we can, and not based on colour prejudice alone."[11] Within a year the Commonwealth Immigrants Act of 1962 was passed which brought primary immigration from the "New Commonwealth" to an end.

The years from 1962 to the end of the 1970s marked a second phase, characterised both by the continual strengthening of the restrictive legislation and by the rise of a variety of racial demagogues and organisations. The Labour Party, which had opposed the 1962 legislation as discriminatory, both renewed it and strengthened it, and their White Paper of 1965 is rightly seen as the foundation document of modern legislative racism. From 1968 we saw the rise and fall of Enoch Powell, whose effective rhetoric raised the racial temperature, and of a range of racist organisations of which the National Front was the most powerful.

The third phase properly begins with Mrs Thatcher's admission, during an interview in January 1978, that she intended to make immigration control a central issue in her election campaign. In this interview she spoke of people being "really rather afraid that this country might be rather swamped by people with a different culture." "The British character" was in danger. When asked if she wished to bring the support which the National Front had been getting back to the Conservative Party, she replied: "Oh very much back, certainly."[12] In the 1979 General Election, the National Front vote collapsed. In 1981 the British Nationality Act created three categories of British citizen, and the years since have seen "nationality" and "Britishness" increasingly interpreted in terms of whiteness.

I want now to reflect on the response of the church to racist movements and ideology and to identify some problems which are, in my view, more pervasive and more deeply rooted in the ecclesiastical mind set. And here I want to avoid two mistaken ways of looking at racial oppression. One is to see racism as so fundamentally different from other forms of oppression that it must be understood and combated in its own right, as an "issue" separate from other issues. To this it must be responded that, while there are indeed unique dimensions to racism, it is important to see the connections and parallels with other levels of oppression, injustice, and discrimination: if this is not possible, then the outlook for any significant attack on these evils is very bleak. However, there is a second approach which links oppressions in such a way as to dissolve them into one another, losing the specific and concrete character of each, and producing a kind of imprecision and conceptual flabbiness which impedes action and induces paralysis. I want to insist both on the specific challenge of racism to Christian faith, and on the connection between this form of oppression and other manifestations of evil. The language of "human oppression" in general must not become an excuse for evading the challenge of the particular experience of racism. Indeed we always move from specific to general: connections can only be made in the midst of struggle about specific issues. So the experience of racism can be a kind of litmus test or barium meal which reveals and exposes other ills within the body politic. What I say therefore about the church's response, or failure to respond, to racism can, *mutatis mutandis*, be applied to a range of social situations.

The first of the problems I wish to identify is the problem of what Henry Clark has termed the "social action curias." Since the 1960s, social curias have developed in most mainstream churches, though their names and functions, as well as their methods, vary: Commissions on Justice and Peace, Boards for Social Responsibility, Task Forces on Human Sexuality, Committees for Social Work, Women's Desks, Divisions for Urban Affairs, and so on. I have worked for, and with, many such bodies, and I do not wish to question the value of much of their work. However, I do question whether they represent the most effective way of responding to injustice, whether racial or otherwise, for a number of reasons.

Such bodies can easily substitute research, monitoring, and lists of recommendations for what I would call "prophetic concreteness." Social action curias are often modelled closely on government departments and corporate institutions, and are subject to the same weaknesses and blind spots. The setting up of yet more working parties which circulate more and more drafts, accumulate more and more discussion papers, and eventually produce lists of recommendations, is a well-established way of delaying response. Much of the research data is already available, much of the ground is already covered, and by the time the report appears, the moment of decision has passed.

But, in addition, such curias can quickly become remote from what is actually happening at the back-street level. Unless there is a continual process of feeding information and sharing of ideas between the grass-roots Christian communities and the bureaucracies, the operations will become remote and top heavy. I get the impression that often the growth of the bureaucratic and managerial sector (not to mention the growing army of consultants, evaluators, and therapists) is at the cost of the decay of the primary Christian cell. So we have a trickle-down approach to social justice, with the added complication that there may be nobody left to receive the trickle since the church has, in many areas of oppression and neglect, been starved out of existence.

The ambiguous role of the trickle-down approach to social doctrine is particularly relevant at this time as we commemorate the centenary of Pope Leo XIII's encyclical *Rerum Novarum* of 15th May 1891, and the fiftieth anniversary of the Malvern Conference of 1941, dominated by the figure and the thought of Archbishop William Temple. Leo's encyclical was the first of a long line of social encyclicals expounding the principles of Catholic social teaching, a list which includes *Quadragesimo Anno* of 1931, *Populorurm Progressio* of 1967, *Laborem Exercens* of 1981 and *Centesimus Annus* of 1991. These encyclicals have sought to relate Catholic social doctrine to changing circumstances, and, while surveys indicate that many Roman Catholics are ignorant of this body of teaching, they are treated with great seriousness by the magisterium.

The Anglican tradition of social thought and social utterance, as expressed in the Malvern Declaration and in other documents associated with William Temple, while it differs in some important ways from the papal encyclicals, does share the trickle-down style. For both *Rerum Novarum* and Malvern, and indeed all the documents which have emerged from the social curia tradition, are essentially statements of general principles handed down by a church magisterium or teaching authority to a constituency whose characteristics are increasingly unclear. What is even less clear is how these general principles relate to actual conflicts of actual Christian communities. And it is here that the challenge of racism exposes the inadequacy of this approach.

For racism does not confront the Christian community in the abstract, as a series of ideological debating points: rather as a threat to its very identity and integrity. It manifests itself in specific forms—racial violence, discriminatory housing allocations, the splitting up of families by entry clearance systems or deportation, economic disempowerment, and so on. It is from the dialectical engagement between concrete experience and gospel truth, not from a detached analysis at committee level, that the church becomes aware of, and responsive to, this threat to its identity.

This raises a second major problem which looms large in the struggle against racism, as it does more generally in the area of social injustice: the problem of liberalism. The critique of the liberal tradition has to begin with the recognition of the positive achievements of that tradition and indeed of its continuing contribution to the theological and political agenda. Nothing I say should be construed as giving support to the currently fashionable use of the term "liberalism" as a pejorative term, an accusation rather than a description. On the contrary, I wish to affirm the value and importance of much in the liberal tradition—its contribution to human potential and human progress, its concern with the self and with human rights, often defending those rights against the values of the dominant social order, and its pragmatism. Theological liberalism, in its Protestant and Catholic forms, has helped to nourish and keep alive the spirit of critical inquiry, openness to new insights, resistance to injustices, and sensitivity to minorities.

However, the liberal tradition, in my view, has four major weaknesses which are exposed particularly when confronted by the monster of racism. First, it operates within a framework of theological optimism, the heir to the eighteenth-century doctrine of progress, and the assumption that improvements and reforms can occur without any fundamental threat to, or break with, the existing system. But this assumption is not at all clear. If racism is not simply a pathological growth upon an otherwise just society, but is deeply rooted within that society, then to attack racism is to threaten the whole fabric. And it is the prospect of so fundamental an upheaval that the liberal Christian often cannot face. Saul Alinsky defined a liberal as a person who leaves the room when an argument turns into a fight.[13] The liberal doctrine of gradual and gentle change has no place for a theology of conflict. As Conrad Noel once put it, it believes that the mighty will be put down from their seats so gently that they will not feel the bump when they hit the ground.[14]

A second problem with the liberal tradition is its concern with the self, with the individual, and with human rights—important concerns, but concerns which can lead to the neglect of the social, economic, and political structures which alone make the exercise of these rights possible and meaningful. The history of liberalism is inseparable from that of individualism, and undoubtedly a passion for individual rights has been important in the struggle against racial discrimination. But I want to argue, with the sociologist William Julius Wilson, that it cannot take us much further: it cannot address the issues of an increasingly fragmented society, of poverty, of economic restructuring, of the loss of moral and social vision.

Thirdly, liberalism continues the trickle-down philosophy, believing that, by exercising a rational and persuasive (and polite) influence on the corridors of power, by identifying and targeting key people in the "policy village," the racial climate will gradually change from above, again without any sign of upheaval and disturbance.

Finally, theological liberalism in particular tends to operate with a bare minimum of doctrinal and spiritual resources, and, when confronted by monsters, this will not do.

Both the strengths and the limitations of the liberal tradition were evident in the era of Archbishop Robert Runcie. Runcie was, I believe, one of the greatest archbishops of the post-war period, and he pushed the liberal tradition to its limits. The late Gary Bennett, in his preface to *Crockfords*, accused Runcie of a "genteel liberalism" and of "nailing his colours to the fence."[15] In fact, Runcie's view of the social order was quite clear, and it comes out in the document *Faith in the City*, the report of the Commission on Urban Priority Areas which he established. While this document was not written by Runcie, it does seem to me faithfully to reflect his approach. The document stands within a long tradition of such documents, going back to the late nineteenth century. They all assume a consensus, a shared good will and sense of the "common good," of common aims between government, church, and people. In the free market and authoritarian climate of Thatcherism, this must have seemed questionable. Nevertheless, Dr. Runcie continued to see the church as a source of moral and spiritual influence within the society and his language was the language of reconciliation.

Faith in the City is a very well-researched document. It draws attention to issues of class and of increasing poverty, it emphasises the growing polarisation in British society, and (unlike most documents from the Church of England) it devotes space—though only five pages—to "minority ethnic groups." Yet a careful study of the document shows that it stands within the liberal tradition. It begins with the regret that Britain is in danger of losing its compassionate character which is "still desired by the majority of its members." It refers at the outset to "basic Christian principles of justice and compassion which we believe we share with the great majority of the people of Britain." And, while it believes that "at present too much emphasis is being given to individualism and not enough to collective obligation," it has no doubt that with a little readjustment, this can be remedied. So it speaks of the need to "redress the balance of the excessive individualism which has crept into both public and private life today."[16] In all of this, there is no suggestion that the evils may be more deeply rooted, more fundamental to the nature of the capitalist order itself, no idea that the values of the Christian tradition may be in conflict with, and not shared by, the bulk of the nation, and no attempt to understand racism other than as a failure to accept black minorities within the assumed parameters of the social structure. The document, in line with liberal understandings of change, operates at the level of gentle persuasion, at the level of the policy village. Church House even borrowed a senior civil servant from the Department of the Environment to service the Commission. And, in line with the liberal theological tradition, it contained little theology—two passing references to the Kingdom of God and one to the Good Samaritan. So, for all its stress on compassion and on advocacy for poor people, it misses something of the heart of gospel conflict.

As both the Runcie and Thatcher decades moved towards their endings, the conceptual horizon of Britain underwent a major, and at points unexpected, shift, a shift towards Europe, and, as the communist regimes began to disintegrate one by one, increasingly towards the notion of a unified Europe. Pope John Paul, on his visit to Poland in June 1979—one month after Mrs Thatcher had come to power—spoke rather prophetically of the "spiritual unity of Europe," going on to warn of the likely resurgence of "age old rivalries"—conflicts between ethnic minorities and the reappearance of nationalism. What to the Pope was a vision of a restored Christendom, marked by Marian shrines and places of pilgrimage, was to Mrs Thatcher an ominous and threatening prospect—a reunified political order with an understanding of sovereignty which was damaging to Britain. But on one aspect Britain and the European Community were at one: in their determination to deal with the issue of migrant labour. Mrs Thatcher even lumped together illegal immigrants, drug traffic, and international terrorism in her Bruges speech of 1988. So, as the flow of Commonwealth immigration to the UK was reduced to a trickle, and as British citizenship for those whose parents and grandparents were not born in the UK became increasingly meaningless, the racial scene has shifted to Europe and to migrant workers with no rights of permanent residence. And, as a large "underclass" of poor migrants has grown up in most European cities, there has been a significant revival of fascist and racist groups in Britain, France, Germany, and elsewhere. The "new racism" is of Pan-European type, and there is a real fear that 1992 will be a year in which "Fortress Europe" will be understood as a common home only for white people.

The fact that it was struggles within Europe and South Africa which most clearly manifested the structural dimensions of racist ideology, and most clearly revealed the hidden potential for resistance within the Christian tradition, raises a third problem in the churches' response to racism: the "problem" of transcendence. One of the assumptions which is still held by many people—though the evidence shows it to be false—is that "radical" theology and "radical" politics go together, while "conservative" theology tends to support the status quo. And, because radicals, on this view, tend to prefer action to worship and prayer, a corollary is that those who give priority to worship and prayer will tend to show little interest in resistance to injustice. And clearly there is some basis for this viewpoint. Yet it is here that the histories of the responses to racism in Nazi Germany and in South Africa throw such a simplistic model into total confusion.

Most theological liberals, as indeed most Christians, in Nazi Germany, found it easy to accommodate to Hitler. The abandonment of those parts of biblical tradition which were seen as "Jewish" helped to undermine any concern for justice, while the fact that many parts of the church had come adrift from their doctrinal roots made it easy for assimilation to the culture of Nazism to occur. Many sermons were preached without any reference to Christian doctrine. The support for Nazism from theologians such as Kittel and Althaus is well known. But the position was far more serious. Richard Gutteridge has shown that from 1879 to 1950 there was no evidence that most Christians in Germany saw any connection between their faith and the issues of race and antisemitism.[17]

However, the resistance, when it came, was led by orthodox believers such as Karl Barth and Dietrich Bonhoeffer, people steeped in Christological reflection, people who emphasised the transcendence of God and the Lordship of Christ, and therefore people whose theology came into collision with state racism. No one in the modern period has emphasised more than Bonhoeffer the need for prayer, worship, and corporate spiritual disciplines. When Hitler came to power, Bonhoeffer was writing a book on Christology: on the surface an irrelevant activity. Yet it was from this material that the churches drew much ammunition for the fight against Nazism. The Nazi experience must lead us to rethink the relation between orthodoxy and resistance to injustice and oppression.

To turn to the South African situation is to see the power of a theologically orthodox worshipping community in conflict with the monster of racism. Allan Boesak's book of meditations, *Comfort and Protest*,[18] uses the symbolism of the Book of Revelation as a resource for a conflict which he sees as fundamentally spiritual. Celebration, worship, and singing are of central importance in this conflict. Boesak's Christianity is deeply biblical with a strong emphasis on the prophetic tradition and on the power of the preached Word.

Or we can look at that long line of witnesses from Michael Scott, Trevor Huddleston, and Ambrose Reeves in the 1940s and 1950s to Desmond Tutu, people shaped by the sacramental theology of the Oxford Movement and particularly by the doctrine of the church as a visible community. Within the South African context, that doctrine was seen as subversive. John Davies has written:

> The most powerful weapon in Catholicism's armoury of imagery in the struggle against injustice is the doctrine of the Body of Christ. . . . There has been nothing radical or intellectually daring about this: the South African situation has required Catholicism to be thoroughly conservative and oppose the moral nonsense of upstart racism with a traditional orthodoxy which insists that there must be a visible fellowship of believers and that Christian love must be acted out in visible terms.[19]

I cite these two examples not to suggest that Christian orthodoxy and resistance to injustice are easily or inevitably related, or to deny that resistance is frequently rooted elsewhere than in this tradition: but to raise the points that there are powerful resources within Christian tradition whose toxicity is only realised in situations of struggle; and that in such situations of struggle, our allies do not always turn out to be the people we expected.

I want therefore to conclude by looking at each of these problems as both a challenge and an opportunity to move beyond the limited frames of reference which they present. I believe that it is essential, in the centenary year of *Rerum Novarum* and in the fiftieth anniversary year of the Malvern Conference, that we recognise that they represent a woefully inadequate expression of the Christian social conscience. Lofty statements from on high may have their place. It is certainly useful to use such statements, whether from past or present Christian leaders, as a constant reminder to them or their successors of their own commitments. Conrad Noel in the early 1900s, and Dorothy Day in the 1930s, used statements from the Fathers and the Popes with great effect in their campaigns. But at the end of the day the Christian struggle against racism and all forms of injustice cannot take place in the board rooms of the managerial radicals but only at the base, where the pain is. And one of my greatest fears is that the Christian community at the base, that primary cellular fabric of Christian consciousness and action, is being starved of resources at the very point at which it is most beset by the monsters of racism, of poverty, of violence, and of despair: while the armies of managers and bureaucrats, assisted by consultants, evaluators, counsellors, and therapists grow by the hour. I do not believe that a church which is top heavy with Fabian type "experts" is in any strong position to combat racism or to engage in any serious struggles. The energy and vision for resistance can come only from strengthened Christian communities at the level of the back streets.

In the same way, we need, while recognising the positive achievements of the liberal tradition, to move beyond liberalism to a greater awareness of the place of conflict in the struggle for justice and peace. One of the real problems in theological liberalism is that it tends to engage with issues from ten miles above the battle. It operates at the level of working parties, task forces, and commissions which consider, sift, assess, and evaluate the data, and it then produces a set of ideas. But because it has not been involved in the ferment, the turbulence, the pain, and the perplexity at the base, liberalism is not able to be involved with the actual process of change. It is for this reason that many church pronouncements, and much writing based on this liberal model, are very vague and non-specific.

I want to propose a different model: that of the disciplined, prayerful, listening Christian community, located in a specific place, which tries to understand and respond to the challenges of its immediate context. It begins in its own back yard, and seeks to use theological and other resources from elsewhere. Connections with other struggles and with wider issues must be made, but they can be made only in the course of activity. Such a model has distinct advantages over the social action curia model: it is rooted in the worshipping and corporate life of actual communities; it begins with concrete and specific issues and moves outwards; and it overcomes the syndrome of a facile optimism in which we seek to deal with problems over too wide an area, at the level of general principles and moral rhetoric, and then gradually move to a cosmic pessimism, which abandons any hope of change of any kind.

Most of all, we need to avoid, and indeed reject, the false polarities of worship and work, liturgy and life, sacraments and social action, piety and politics. In combating racism we are confronted with principalities and powers, with spiritual forces of evil, with the attack on human dignity and human liberty which is portrayed in Scripture under the symbols of Babylon and the dragon. We are in fact faced with the birth of a monster, and we need to heed Nietzsche's warning that those who fight with monsters are in danger of turning into monsters. It is therefore of the greatest importance that we draw on all the resources for spiritual warfare that are available. It was David Jenkins who coined the term "spirituality for combat," and it is an urgent need now when so many Christian people are experiencing exhaustion, burnout, despair, and severe undernourishment. But there is another aspect. If John Davies is correct in his diagnosis of the South African situation, the struggle for racial justice cannot take place purely at the level of the mind, the conquest of ignorance, or at the level of the streets, the conquest of territorial space, important as these things are. It must also, and most importantly, take place at the level of the creation of communities of dissent, communities of justice, communities of the creatively maladjusted. Sharon Welch sees very clearly that it is here that Christian truth is tested.

> The truth of Christian faith is at stake not in terms of its coherence with ontological structures and their potential modifications, but in life and death struggles. . . . It is in this arena of the determination of the character of daily life that the truth of Christian faith, both in its method and referent, must be determined. The battle against nihilism and oppression is not primarily conceptual but practical. The focus therefore of a liberating faith and of theology is not primarily the analysis of human being and its possibilities but the creation of redeemed communities.[20]

So I want to suggest that, in confronting racism, we are confronting an alternative gospel, an alternative explanation of what it is to be human, a fundamental threat to the nature and identity of the Christian community. And in the same way as Benedict, and later Bonhoeffer, created structures of holiness and justice which could be a focus for resistance to and transcendence of the dark ages ahead of them, so the struggle for human integrity and human community today is inseparable from that for a renewed spirituality. Yet the recovery of spirituality in the late twentieth century is not without its dangers, and it is to this that I want to move in Chapter Two.

2
Comfort or Transformation?: the Crisis of Modern Spirituality

In Chapter One I suggested that it was essential to all good theological work that there be a dialectical encounter between the tradition and concrete, lived experience. I want now to look at the question of spirituality as it has arisen in my adult life and ministry. I was ordained in 1964, the year after the publication of John Robinson's *Honest to God*. At that time it was not uncommon for rectors of parishes to come to the seminary wringing their hands in despair about their new curates. "My curate doesn't pray, doesn't regard worship, silence, the daily office, as important, and seems only to want to rush around being relevant." By the time that I was on the staff of a seminary in the 1970s, we were seeing almost the reverse process: newly ordained deacons returning to the seminary after a few months in a parish, wringing their hands in despair about their rectors. "My rector doesn't pray. How can I get it across to him that when I want time for silence, prayer, retreat, I am not some kind of spiritual freak?" A simple explanation of the change would, of course, be that the curates of the 1960s had become the rectors of the 1970s—and hadn't changed. However, I think more had been happening. Some would say that a new generation had turned aside in weariness from the struggles of the 1960s and were now engaged in a quest for enriched, deepened spiritual foundations for their activity. But the activism of the 1960s has been greatly exaggerated, and most Christian people were not affected.

Nevertheless, whatever the causes, there has been a resurgence of spirituality. Spirituality is in again. But we need to be very cautious before we welcome it uncritically. We need to ask: Is it a diversion, a compartment, a commodity, yet another subject to be studied? Is it Christian? That may seem a silly question, but it is important. There is no interest shown in spirituality in the Bible: the stress is more on building up the Body of Christ, and on the corporate life of the people of God. Much spirituality is not Christian. Some of it is anti-Christian, including much which occurs within a Christian context. So we need to ask: Is it wholesome? Does it contribute to the building up of the Body of Christ or not? The spiritual world is not universally benign: we need to test the spirits, to ask the question: Is this true spirituality or false?

Between *Honest to God* and the spiritual renewal of the present day there occurred that decade called "The Sixties." Between 1967 and 1971 I worked in Soho, in the West End of London, and there I found myself at the heart of the counter-culture. Many of the people who came my way were "meta-hippies," people who had moved from drugs to spirituality. There seemed to be two ways of interpreting this phenomenon. Some said that they had simply moved from drugs to spirituality: the drug experience had led them to the spiritual quest. Others argued rather that a spiritual revival was inevitable, and had got side-tracked for a while into drugs. However it was interpreted, it was clear that a religious revival was occurring among some young people and it mainly bypassed the Christian tradition.

There are two important features to note here. First, it is easy to exaggerate the significance of what was taking place in those years. As an unfriendly critic of my own work wrote: "Life in Burslem, Tadcaster and Crewe was not greatly affected."[1] It is easy to generalise on the basis of limited data from San Francisco and London. But, secondly, whatever was the case twenty years ago, the spiritual revival is now more widespread, and much of it has become commonplace.

In my case, the demand for spiritual direction came originally from non-Christians. It was young people with no connections with organised religion who were searching for the transcendent. Their perspective was expressed well in a small book published in 1967:

> We live in a secular world. To adapt to this world the child abdicates its ecstasy. . . . Having lost our experience of the spirit, we are expected to have faith. But this faith comes to be a belief in a reality which is not evident. There is a prophecy in Amos that there will be a time when there will be a famine in the land, not a famine for bread nor a thirst for water, but of *hearing* the words of the Lord. That time has now come to pass. It is the present age.[2]

In writing that, Ronnie Laing bore witness to the fact that there was a widespread dissatisfaction with the famine which he described. In writing those words, he summed up the spiritual climate of that decade.

I believe that the 1960s are of crucial importance in the recent history of spiritual renewal. It is most important that we do not follow the conventional right-wing trend and write off this decade as a detour, but that we recognise both its creative potential and its limitations, and build upon it.

However, the resurgence of spirituality has been a mixed blessing. In 1973 I identified much of the current spiritual quest as a new gnosticism,[3] and nothing that has occurred subsequently has caused me to revise this view. Indeed, subsequent events have strengthened my belief. What do I mean by gnosticism? The gnostic tradition seems to have three main features.

Gnosticism

First, it contains a determination to locate evil in matter and to create a dualism of spirit and matter. So the realm of the spirit is circumscribed within narrow limits, becoming "the spiritual dimension" or "the inner life." The aim of the spiritual person is to ascend, detached from the messy concerns of earth, to a higher, more spiritual realm. There is a paradox in relation to sexuality, identified most of all with sin in the gnostic tradition. Many gnostics reject sexuality altogether as a symptom of the Fall. Thus the wonderful entry in one dictionary under the heading *Encratites*: "an early Christian sect which believed that original sin was transmitted by sexual intercourse. Extinct." However, in tandem with this ascetic tradition, there is also the theme in gnosticism that the spiritual person is above the moral law. Sexual liberation becomes a symbol of total liberation. Thus one finds throughout the history of the gnostic movements a recurring combination of otherworldliness and sexual excess. And what is true of sex is true generally: it is common to find otherworldliness and extreme worldliness combined.

Secondly, there is a stress on spiritual technology and on the geography of the higher realms. Gnostic movements tend to become obsessed with the acquisition of techniques and methodologies. Self-cultivation replaces the vision of God. Even spiritual direction is seen as the cult of the expert. And there is a good deal of concern with the spectacular and with trivial manifestations of spiritual power, what Roszak has called "the lumpen occult version of Abbott and Costello meet Jehovah."[4]

Thirdly, gnostics divide the world into two groups, the initiates and the common herd. To be spiritual is to be part of an elite, to possess a higher consciousness, to belong to the community of the *illuminati*, the enlightened ones, the true believers.

Christian orthodoxy comes into conflict with this approach to spirituality at all three points. First, Christian orthodoxy insists that the material world and its structures are the vehicle of the divine, the raw material of sanctification. It cannot therefore abandon the struggle for a transfigured world, or see earthly struggles as separate from spiritual struggles.

Secondly, Christian orthodoxy is rooted in the belief in salvation by grace, not by technique or method. It is God centred, not self centred.

Thirdly, Christian orthodoxy stresses that grace is common. It is concerned with the common life of the Body of Christ and cannot be elitist or esoteric.

I think as a historian. I believe that Christianity is a faith uniquely rooted in historical events, and that it is important to nourish a sense of history if we are to have a sound perspective on most issues. Much currently fashionable spirituality, and much writing on pastoral care, has no sense of history, and seems to be at the mercy of every passing fad and fashion.

In Chapter One I suggested that, in the conflict with injustice, a rootedness in a community of resistance, solidarity, and commitment is vital. This is not a time for lonely wilderness crusaders. Similarly I want to suggest that the search for roots, for a living tradition, is a necessary part of the struggle for a viable and nourishing spirituality, and that much of the current spiritual quest can be understood best in terms of the recovery of the meaning of Christian community. To be a Christian at all is to be grafted into a living tradition, the Body of Christ, and that tradition is historically rooted. So I want to look at the contemporary crisis of spirituality by looking briefly at the roots of that crisis in the nineteenth century.

The nineteenth century was marked by religious revivals of many kinds, but four overlapping movements are of importance in understanding some of the problems of our current revival. The first is the concern with holiness, sanctification, which stretches from Wesley through the Holiness Movement, with its concern for the ''higher Christian

life," to the outbreak of Pentecostalism. The Wesleyan
revival represented both a liberation of the emotions and
a rediscovery of the energy and exuberance of the Spirit,
and a new emphasis on the need for the Christian community to be a community of holiness. "Entire sanctification"
was the heart of Wesley's teaching, and this manifested itself
in the band meetings, the class meetings, and the stress on
spiritual discipline, on method, from which the movement
took its name. This concern with holiness was not individualist or elitist, for Wesley was passionately concerned for
the common people, and insisted that there was "no holiness but social holiness."[5] The links between Methodism
and the early trade union movement also meant that in some
places the concern with holiness was linked with the concern for justice.

It was from the Wesleyan concern with sanctification, with
the "second blessing," that the Holiness Movement developed around C.G. Finney and Oberlin College, and Whea-
ton, with a commitment to promote the "higher Christian
life"; and it was out of the Holiness tradition—as well as
in reaction to aspects of it—that classical Pentecostalism
began as the twentieth century dawned. Donald Dayton in
his *Theological Roots of Pentecostalism*[6] shows that early
Methodism provided the crucial theological foundation for
the recovery of the doctrine of the Spirit which was the central feature of the Pentecostal revival. The whole tradition
from Wesley to Pentecostalism was also, of course, a musi-
cal tradition, expressed as much in hymns as in preaching.

There was, running roughly parallel with the Holiness
tradition, another tradition which was also concerned with
holiness: the Oxford Movement which had begun in 1833
and, by the 1850s, was transforming the face of the Church
of England. "My Lord, I saw three men in green,"
exclaimed the chaplain to the Bishop of London after a visit
to St Alban's Church, Holborn, "and I do not think they
will quickly be put down." The chaplain had witnessed one

aspect of this religious revival: the revival of rite and ceremony as an aspect of the recovery of the Holy. For the Oxford Movement was also concerned with holiness and with spiritual deepening. Much of its activity can be viewed as a rejection of the dreary, conformist, and culturally uncritical religion of the "Tory party at prayer" kind of Anglicanism. Against this it insisted on the spiritual autonomy of the church. With the Oxford Movement came the return of sacramental confession, books of personal devotion, retreats, churches which were open as places of prayer, and a strong emphasis on "the beauty of holiness." Richard Holloway has spoken of "a converting aesthetic" at the heart of the movement.

> Dostoievsky said that beauty would redeem the world, and the builders and artists of the Catholic revival seemed to have cherished the same truth. The churches of the Revival have a powerful quality about them that suggests spiritual reality, the other world, the other country. There is something about these churches that draws us to our knees. They were never simply meeting places for worship, or for listening to preaching or teaching. They were shrines, holy places that spoke of God. In an almost miraculous way they did and do their own thing and had and have a strange sweet converting power.[7]

It was the fusion of the sacramentalism and ritualism of the Oxford Movement with the social and incarnational theology of F. D. Maurice which produced the phenomenon often referred to as "Anglo-Catholic socialism" towards the end of the nineteenth century and the early years of the twentieth century, a movement associated with Stewart Headlam, Charles Marson, Conrad Noel, and, later, with Maurice Reckitt, Percy Widdrington, and many others. It is a serious mistake to see this movement, as some do, as a purely political movement or, in its milder versions, as social reform with a vaguely religious colouring. It was deeply theological and spiritual, and it sought a unity between the world of the sacraments and the world of the streets. Donald Gray in his book *Earth and Altar*[8] shows that it was in Anglo-Catholic socialism, and particularly in the work of Percy Dearmer, that the origins of the parish communion are to be found.

But, in contrast to the ritualists, for whom the sacramental world was often a retreat from harsh reality, a world of devotion and personal piety, the sacramental socialists saw the Eucharist as the celebration of a new world. "Those who assist at Holy Communion," wrote Stewart Headlam, "are bound to be holy communists."[9] Father Adderley described Headlam's view of the Sunday Eucharist as "the weekly meeting of a society of rebels against a Mammon worshipping world order."[10]

For those early Christian radicals, worship and struggle went together, and along with worship and struggle went joy, mirth, and dancing. Headlam's licence to officiate was removed by the Bishop of London and never restored because of his support for the ballet and the music hall. At Thaxted Church under Conrad Noel the Morris dancing on the village green was crucial to the spirituality and social consciousness of the parish. There was far more here than romanticism and nostalgia: there was a sense of joy and liberation, of the unity of piety and politics in the common life of common people.

Finally, at the end of the nineteenth century, a movement of reaction, which had been gathering momentum for some time, became consolidated under the name "fundamentalism." The word was not used until 1920 though the volume called *The Fundamentals* was issued earlier. There has been much discussion of fundamentalism recently. Its relevance to my theme is that it represented an early "closing of the American mind." In origin it was an American movement, a deeply spiritual movement, but a movement characterised by a defensive posture (against liberalism, socialism, and Darwinism) and by a desire for certainty and the exclusion of doubt. In this it is similar to gnosticism. But with fundamentalism the truth ceases to be a way of life, a journey, and becomes a weapon. Doubt is excluded in this closed system of absolute certainty.

I believe that in the first three movements we were witnessing, in various ways, movements of liberation—liberation of the emotions, liberation of church from state, the gospel itself as a liberating force. In the fourth we were witnessing a movement of foreclosure, of repression, of what Alice Walker called the "colonising of the spirit." The crucial spiritual characteristic of fundamentalism is this attempt to close off the boundaries, to capture and control, to exclude doubt and darkness.

Now as Marx reminded us in *The 18th Brumaire of Louis Bonaparte*, it is out of our old history that our new history is made, and the spiritual movements which have characterised the years since the 1960s have built upon these earlier traditions. The growth of Neo-Pentecostalism, or charismatic renewal, since 1967 has revived Wesley's concern with a holy people, with enthusiasm and joy, and with the old Holiness emphasis on "the second blessing," and "the higher Christian life." The distinctive marks of Pentecostalism, in its classical and newer versions, have been the gifts of the Spirit (especially tongues but also healing), stress on Scripture, spontaneity in worship, and evangelism. The earlier emphasis on the Second Coming seems to have been played down.

I think we need to be very careful in evaluating the effects of Neo-Pentecostal spirituality. It has certainly, in some of its appearances, exhibited evidence of elitism, sentimentality, bad theology (expressed in even worse hymns and liturgy); a withdrawal from serious analysis, thought, and action; and a tendency to escape from serious engagement beneath the facade of the cliché-ridden jargon and the fixed charismatic smile. On the other hand, we have seen the signs of holiness, of real community, the rediscovery of what it is to celebrate, to rejoice, to praise, to be the Body of Christ, and for many this movement has represented a real liberation from dead religion into the freedom of the children of God.

But there is one aspect of Pentecostal spirituality which is of fundamental importance for the future, and it connects with my comments in the previous chapter. On a world scale, Pentecostalism is a black and Third World Christian movement. In the USA and Britain, Pentecostalism represents the largest tradition of black Christianity, and the only form of Christianity developed and led by black people. The fastest growing churches in England are black Pentecostal ones. The coming together of Pentecostal spirituality and the radical black liberation tradition is evident in both the USA and Britain as well as further afield. Within a mile of the scene of Spike Lee's film *Do the Right Thing* stands the House of the Lord which, under the leadership of Pastor Herbert Daughtry, reflects a radical form of Pentecostalism which is likely to increase in significance as we enter the twenty-first century.

The spiritual agenda of the Oxford Movement included the revival of the centrality of the Eucharist, personal devotion, the use of the daily offices, retreats, confession, and, later, spiritual direction. Many of these have now been absorbed into the life of many sections of the church. We have the Oxford Movement to thank for much that is now taken for granted. Much of the work of the Second Vatican Council was anticipated by Charles Gore, Henry Scott Holland, and Michael Ramsey.

It is when we look at the third of the nineteenth-century movements that we must wonder what has become of its project of integration. The early radicalism of Headlam and his disciples was not a freak phenomenon, but was rooted in a theology of the common life. Michael Ramsey in *From*

Gore to Temple[11] described the spread of this tradition of incarnational and sacramental theology in which spirituality and social struggle were united. However, it was only the ritual side of the movement which was exported to the USA, where Anglo-Catholicism has tended to become precious, exotic, correct, and dainty. The radical tradition seems to have withered and died. So we need to ask: Does Anglo-Catholicism today represent an exhausted religious tradition? Is it living on its past? Certainly in many of its manifestations, it seems to carry a ghetto consciousness, cut off from the central concerns of the Christian world, looking backwards to some fictitious golden age. However there can be no doubt that fundamentalism is alive and well, not least in its Catholic forms.

In looking at these four movements with origins in the nineteenth century, we need to become aware of the different purposes that a spiritual revival can serve, and the different directions it may take. For example, what is it that changes a movement with its roots among poor people—such as early Methodism and early Pentecostalism—into a movement of respectability and conformity to whose values poor people are a threat? What is it which leads a sacramental tradition into a privatised piety, contrary to its essential social character? What are the factors which lead to elitism, first-and second-class Christians, ''holy huddles,'' and inward-looking communities? And where lies the appeal of fundamentalism in all its forms? Spirituality is a mixed blessing. Spiritual growth in itself is not a value. Without careful cultivation, growth produces no livable human environment, but only the deadly luxuriance of swamp or jungle.

I want therefore to conclude this chapter by raising the question: What kind of spirituality is needed for the twenty-first century? And I want to begin to answer this question by locating the crisis of modern spirituality as one of comfort or transformation. Crisis? What crisis? Is there a crisis?

Yes, there is a crisis, a judgment, a call for discernment, a turning point where spirituality could hive off into a realm of its own. Valerie Pitt, commenting on the Oxford Movement, has said that, "the Tractarians unconsciously made religion a life substitute rather than a life revealer, not a way into the splendours of the visible world but a way out. That habit of mind is fixed in us still and ultimately it is destructive of religion itself."[12] I do not think that process is unique to the Anglo-Catholic tradition, and it represents a crisis.

Nor do I want to deny that comfort is needed. The question is: Is the main purpose of "the spiritual life" to provide comfort, reassurance, new sources of inspiration to improve our lives? Or is it to challenge, confront, and transform our lives? Jim Wallis of the Sojourners Community has complained that in much modern evangelism Jesus comes into our lives not to transform us, but simply to improve us. Miguez-Bonino made a similar point when he said that many people seemed to look to religion to satisfy them, not to transform them.[13]

In Chapter One I quoted Sharon Welch who said that Christian faith is at stake in life and death struggles. The focus of a liberating faith, she argued, must be the creation of redeemed communities. What would be the marks of such communities?

First, they would be *baptismal communities*, communities which would take seriously and seek to live out the renunciation of the world, the turning to Christ, and the cleansing and sanctifying power of the Spirit which are at the heart of the baptismal liturgy. A baptismal spirituality would stress the continuing conflict with the structures of oppression and injustice, the continuing call to conversion, to *metanola*, and the continuing availability of God's grace. I do not believe that work for justice will get very far unless we locate it at the very centre of Christian existence, that is, in the baptismal covenant.

Secondly, they would be *eucharistic communities*. The

parish communion movement has been a good movement, but there is a danger of fellowship at the expense of awe, which, as Evelyn Underhill said, is a type of religion which does not wear well.[14] The liturgy needs not only to reinforce bonds of solidarity but also to point to glory, to new possibilities. Part of the power of eucharistic worship is its ability to raise the imagination to a vision of a world transfigured and to provide the resources to help make that vision real. A eucharistic spirituality would emphasise the commonness of spirituality, a spirituality rooted in the physical crudity of incarnation, resurrection, and eucharist, and also the mystery and wonder of God's Kingdom into whose life we are caught up. Eucharistic worship is about glory: the very word "orthodox" means right glory, right *doxa*.

Thirdly, they would be *communities of "biblical people."* Part of the strength of Anglicanism lies in its knowledge of the Scriptures, its praying of the Scriptures, and its sense of the wholeness of the Scriptures. Much modern spirituality is very dubiously biblical. It has, for example, lost the commitment to justice and mercy of the Hebrew prophets. Christian spirituality must be rooted in the memory, the *anamnesis* of Jesus Christ, in the saving history of his death and resurrection.

Fourthly, they would be *communities of rational inquiry*. Alasdair MacIntyre has shown that there can be no justice, no rationality, in the abstract, but only in relation to specific traditions.[15] The tradition of Christian spirituality to which I am committed is a spirituality of struggle, of interrogation, a community of debate, a zone of truth seeking.

Fifthly, they will be *inclusive communities*. By this I do not simply refer to inclusive language but to inclusive people. Are the poor at home? Who is left out? In the ministry of Jesus the centrality of the meal is clear, but so also is the fact of the company he kept—riff-raff, the ritually impure, outcasts, people of dubious morals.

Finally, they will be *communities of expectation, of vision*.

Walter Brueggemann sees the aim of liturgy, of pastoral care, and of community under the Scriptures to include the nourishing of alternative vision, prophetic imagination, the ministry of keeping alive the flame of renewal, the hope of transformation, the vision of God.[16]

All these features have been present in the emphasis on spiritual renewal which has marked liberation theology since Gustavo Gutierrez's plea in 1973 for a spirituality of liberation.[17] Most of the significant writing since then has been Christological or concerned with the spiritual journey and with spiritual disciplines for the struggle against oppression. We have seen similar developments in the spirituality which has grown up among women and around the creation. It is not clear how much of this explosion can be contained within conventional channels. Christian spirituality is messy, incomplete, not a closed system. It is open to the future, to vision. More than anything we need to recover the sense of vision.

Above all this, though, there hovers a massive question mark. Is the church so tidy, so programmed, so managerial and bureaucratic, so organised for efficiency and success, that none of this can happen? If my analysis in the previous chapter is correct, we have good cause to worry about the erosion of any distinct identity. Has the church abandoned vision and struggle, for peace, and harmony, and security? If so, we have good cause to worry. Has it preferred comfort and a quiet life to transformation and challenge? We need to remember Tawney's words about the Fabians: ''They tidy the room but they open no windows in the soul.''[18] That is the dilemma which faces us today.

3
The Future: towards a Subversive Orthodoxy

In his book *Deity and Domination* David Nicholls comments: ''Works whose titles begin with the word 'Towards' are not calculated to inspire confidence in the authors' ability to reach their appointed goal.''[1] I take the point. However, I believe it is better to start a journey whose end is unclear than to stand still. For, as the Red Queen in *Alice* and St Bernard agreed, to stand still is to go backwards. Christian faith is justified or negated, vindicated or crushed, not in theory but in the course of movement. In the 1960s a series of theological books with nautical titles appeared, initiated by Alec Vidler's *Soundings*, and followed by *Four Anchors from the Stern* and *Praying for Daylight*, while the inimitable Eric Mascall wrote *Up and Down in Adria*. All these books were based on Paul's shipwreck in Acts 27. What much of this writing missed was that the purpose of taking soundings is to aid navigation, and that it is only in the process of navigation, of movement, that we make progress either in sailing or in understanding the world. I believe that faith is an aid to navigation, that orthodoxy is about movement, and that Christian spirituality is a spirituality for people on the move. As Augustine says, we sing Alleluia and we keep on walking.[2] To stand still is a recipe for fossilisation, while those who are tempted to nostalgia and to a backward-looking stance should remember the sad fate of Mrs Lot.

So I'm talking about exploration. I'm talking about pilgrimage. I'm talking about orthodoxy as a journey, involving risks, dangers, and vulnerability. I'm talking about wilderness and exile, and, in Arnold Wesker's words, "I'm talking about Jerusalem." I am suggesting that, while the journey calls for traditional and well-tested resources, we also learn and unlearn much en route. And we don't know how the journey will end.

But this is not how orthodoxy is seen in many quarters today. Anyone who has sat through debates at church conferences and conventions will be only too well aware that the language is increasingly coded. I recently heard a resolution at a diocesan convention which called on members to assert their belief in the orthodox faith as revealed in the Holy Scriptures—on the surface an entirely proper thing to do (although, as one member pointed out, they had only recently reaffirmed the baptismal covenant which put the matter more adequately.) But I got a strong feeling that this resolution was not simply a statement but rather a weapon to be used at some future date against certain groups (in this case, I suspect, homosexuals). Orthodoxy has become a word surrounded by fear, anxiety, and the siege mentality, and discussions about it are marked by defensiveness. Orthodoxy and indeed "the moral order"—the two are often confused—are seen as fragile plants. It will take only a liberal gust of wind to blow them over. Or, to change the metaphor, orthodoxy is seen as like King Canute, positioned vigorously against the oncoming tide.

Now there is a certain truth in this kind of language. Athanasius *contra mundum* does stand for something important in our history. But Athanasius was dynamic, creative, a pioneer as well as a synthesiser. I know of no movement which has made progress and been a converting and transformative force which has been based on negative positions and on oppositional stances alone. Such movements tend to attract bitter, negative, backward-looking people, and become a kind of rump, and often a species of religious fascism.

I have the impression that the coding and increased polarising, not to mention distortion, of language is something which has done particular damage to the Anglican tradition. So a tradition which was once known for the creative and pioneering nature of its thought, for the comprehensive character of its vision, and for the theological balance and wholeness of its worship and life, seems increasingly characterised by fragmentation, narrowness, and lack of creativity. One symptom of this is the current tendency in both the church and the secular media to use the word "traditionalist" in a deeply untraditional way. I sometimes feel that a traditionalist means one who is effectively ignorant of the tradition in its richness and complexity but who clings, neurotically and fiercely, to the conventions of several decades past. I even saw the clerical collar described recently as traditional although it was introduced in the nineteenth century by the Rosminian priest Luigi Gentili and was unknown to the church for most of its life. On the other hand, a friend of mine who recently resigned from the faculty of a well-known traditionalist seminary in the Episcopal Church complained of the lack of interest shown there in the study of Hebrew, Greek, and Latin! Traditional?

It would be instructive in this connection to pull off from the shelves Conrad Noel's little book *Socialism in Church History*, published in 1910. Noel, the fiery parish priest of Thaxted in Essex, expresses his amusement that so many Christians appealed to "the Fathers" on relatively minor matters of church order and discipline, but ignored their teaching on the weightier matters of justice and equality. He was particularly struck by the fact that the appeal to the Fathers often came from "a High Churchman who is continually appealing to tradition on questions of scents and vestments and on every kind of doctrinal issue." Noel commented: "He has appealed to the Fathers: to the Fathers he shall go."[3] If one opens oneself up to the tradition, one must be prepared for some shocks and surprises.

It is essential then to distinguish orthodoxy from conventionality, traditionalism from conservatism. Stanley Evans used to argue that Christianity is such a powerful, subversive, and, in the climate of a culture geared to violence and exploitation, extremely dangerous force that it has to be tamed, watered down, and house trained. So the power of a liberating orthodoxy gives way to the conformity of conventional religion. One needs therefore to look for orthodoxy on the margins, at the points of resistance to the culture. In the North American context we might turn to William Stringfellow's essay of 1964 on "The orthodoxy of radical involvement,"[4] every bit as relevant now as when he wrote it.

Indeed one of the most peculiar aberrations of the present day is the notion that political involvement is somehow unorthodox and is a result of liberalism. One might usefully recall the words of the great Anglican social thinker Maurice Reckitt as long ago as 1935.

> If you had told any typical Christian thinker in any century from the twelfth to the sixteenth that religion had nothing to do with economics, and that bishops must not intrude in these matters upon the deliberations of laymen—propositions which to many of the correspondents to our newspapers appear to be axiomatic—he would either have trembled for your faith or feared for your reason. He would have regarded you, in short, as either a heretic or a lunatic.[5]

But just as we need to distinguish a living orthodoxy from dreary convention and conformity, and tradition from conservatism, so I believe that we need to move beyond both fundamentalism and liberalism. Liberalism has many positive achievements to its credit, but it is deficient in its adherence to individualism, in its commitment to gradual reform within the system, and in the inadequacy and weakness of its theological base. Fundamentalism is important in its insistence on "the fundamentals" but it has become a form of closure, a packaged approach to religion, a deep-freeze theology. There is no leeway, no space for creativity, for darkness, for exploration. Nor is the problem here one which is peculiar to Christianity. Bhikhu Parekh, writing from a Hindu background, has argued that much religious life is polarised "between holy text and moral void."[6] So many religious people have come to believe that it is only by holding tenaciously and literally to the sacred writings, the foundational documents, that we can avoid moral collapse and emptiness. Is there a middle way?

At this point let me allude briefly to the question of postmodernism, on which it could be said that "of making books there is no end." Some see the shift from modernity, when all was known, to postmodernity as a shift to doubt, disorder, and fragmentation, to a position where, in Jean Baudrillard's words, all we can do is "play with the pieces." Fredric Jameson presents a critical view of postmodernism as a superstructure generated by late capitalism, the capitalism of multinationals, mass media, and information technology, and he identifies much of this culture as decentred and schizophrenic.[7] Other writers see in the postmodern rejection of the fixity and rigidity of knowledge—as in quantum theory and the scientific recognition of the indeterminate and elusive character of reality—a new and hopeful climate in which religious traditions, along with other traditions and communities of inquiry, can find a voice and receive a hearing. Sandra Schneiders, for instance, suggests that the liberal era of historical criticism has run its course, and that now the dialogue between text and person can begin. The signs, she claims, are very hopeful though she has some questions about the Bible.[8]

It is important to be clear that what is being discussed cannot be understood within the models of liberalism. Those are the models of a previous period. Richard Neuhaus sums up the positions in this way.

> Preliberals assume that doctrines are propositions that express revealed and therefore unchanging truths. Liberals assume that doctrines are symbolic expressions of universal and unchanging religious experiences. Post-liberals incline to the view that doctrines are essentially "rules" reflecting the grammar of specific religious traditions.[9]

However, one of the most frequently asserted claims of the postmodernist period is that which asserts the "collapse of grand narratives." This is a claim which raises profound problems not only for Christianity but also for Marxism, for socialism, and for all religions, ideologies, and claims to any overall, comprehensive view of the world.

So is orthodoxy possible? Or are all orthodoxies in collapse in this new postmodern time of flux and fragmentation? I want to suggest that there are two ways of looking at orthodoxy, and here I draw on some ideas in an essay by Rowan Williams.[10]

The first view sees orthodoxy as a closed system, determined, watertight, a package, a comprehensive ideology, total, complete. We are programmed by it, captured by it, imprisoned within it. It stifles thought and distorts perception. Within its confines no real conversation is possible, and self-scrutiny is banished. Its closest political analogue is the fascist state. And this is no figment: we recognise it, we know it well.

The second way to see orthodoxy is as a tradition of shared speech, shared symbols, a living community of revelation and discourse, a tradition which makes critical engagement

2 VIEWS

possible. Indeed it is only an orthodoxy of this kind which makes critical engagement possible. Tradition is not static but dynamic, not stifling but liberating. Orthodoxy is a tool, not an end. It looks beyond the conceptual climate of the present to its source events and documents, and there is a constant dialogue, a critical encounter, and dialectical relationship, between the received tradition and contemporary insights, experiences, and struggles. It is out of such encounters that significant changes and renewals occur.

In proposing this way of looking at orthodoxy I am rejecting one fashionable approach to contemporary Christian dilemmas, an approach associated with the former Bishop of London, Graham Leonard, and expressed in his Fulton Lecture of 1987.[11] Here Leonard divides the Christian world into a relativist and subjectivist wing which holds that the Christian faith is made up and revised as one goes along, and from time to time brought into conformity with the spirit of the age; and a traditional wing which recognises that the faith has been once for all revealed and is incapable of revision or modification. Now not only do I regard this view as a trivialisation and caricature of the situation, but I think that, even within its own frame of reference, it reduces the range of possible options. It is a caricature. I have never met any Christian—including Bishop Leonard himself—who holds that nothing has been revealed, nor have I met one— including Bishop Leonard—who believes that nothing can be modified. Many traditionalists conform very much to the dominant culture—indeed the extent of their conformism is one reason why orthodoxy and tradition are often equated with conservatism and convention.

But I want to suggest that relativism and revelation, liberalism and fundamentalism, are not the only alternatives: that there is a creative orthodoxy which is not only compatible with, but also of necessity involves, a critical, subversive, movement of interrogation and of resistance, a continuing encounter between things new and old. Indeed

I want to suggest that orthodoxy as perceived and lived in this way is not stifling but inclusive, not fearful but risk taking, not simplistic but rooted in ambiguity and paradox. The rejection of paradox and ambiguity is the characteristic of heretics in all ages as both Irenaeus in the second century and G.K. Chesterton in the twentieth century saw. Heresy is one-dimensional, narrow, over-simplified, and boring. It is straight-line thinking, preferring a pseudo-clarity to the many-sidedness of truth, tidiness to the mess and complexity of reality. Orthodoxy by contrast is rooted and grounded in the unknowable, in the incomprehensible mystery of God. It is ironical that the word *agnosia*, which is so central to the apophatic tradition of eastern Orthodoxy, has come into English as agnostic, often understood as meaning relativist, uncommitted, or lacking in belief. Yet it is the key word in the orthodox tradition of unknowing. Against the heretics who wanted to have reality all sewn up and conceptually clear, orthodox theology pointed to that core of mystery, that dark centre which lies at the heart of faith. The Cappadocian Fathers laboured long over the question of how much could be known and said about the nature of God. Could God be known directly? Could God be named? They concluded that God was known not in his essence but through his energies, through his actions in the world. According to St John of Damascus, God does not exist in the sense that we normally use that word: the whole concept is inapplicable to God since only objects exist and God is not an object. God is known through unknowing, through *agnosia*.

I raise all this because what is often mistaken for orthodoxy today is in fact what orthodox thinkers of the past saw as heresy: the desire to have everything cut and dried, clear and precise, the desire to remove contradictions and ambiguities, the mistaking of the part for the whole. Some would say that the holding together of apparent contradictions and ambiguities is of the very nature of the orthodox project. Eric Mascall in his study *Via Media*[12] argues that orthodoxy is an attempt to hold together unresolved and apparently contradictory truths: transcendence and immanence, divine and human natures, impassibility and passion, and so on. Heresy resolved these contradictions by coming down on one side or the other. Orthodoxy, on the other hand, held contrary truths in tension, defined parameters, and so made further debates, clarifications, expansions, revisions, and dialogue possible. The Council of Chalcedon, for example, did not close the debate on the nature of Christ, but left open the possibility of reflection, thought, and debate.

At the heart of the orthodox approach is the theme of mystery and of the symbolic. The word symbol comes from a Greek root which means "thrown together." Orthodoxy is inseparable from mystery and symbol, and these are different from puzzles and problems. Puzzles exist in order to be solved, problems are soluble at least in principle. Mysteries have no solution, nor can symbols be translated into concepts. Mysteries are lived into, symbols swallow us whole. So to be orthodox is to enter into mystery.

I want now to propose the outrageous suggestion that there could be, within the lost, neglected, and under-used resources of the Anglican tradition, the potential for a creative and dynamic orthodoxy. I want to approach this first by restating two questions which were raised long ago by G. K. Chesterton. According to Chesterton, many sections of the church are asking, "How much can Mr Jones swallow?" In fact, he says, the important question is: "What does Mr Jones need to eat?" There is a minimalism in much liberal Christianity which asks: How much can we do without, and not suffer from malnutrition or starvation? The orthodox question is rather: What resources are available to provide adequate nourishment, enjoyment, exhilaration, and interior energy for the massive struggles ahead?

In 1934 Reinhold Niebuhr wrote a remarkable study called

Reflections on the End of an Era in which he said: [REINHOLD NIEBUHR]

> The liberal culture of modernity is quite unable to give adequate guidance and direction to a confused generation which faces the disintegration of a social system and the task of building a new one. In my opinion, adequate spiritual guidance can only come through a more radical political orientation and more conservative religious convictions than are comprehended in the culture of our era. The effort to combine political radicalism with a more classical and historical interpretation of religion will strike the modern mind as bizarre and capricious. It will satisfy neither the liberals in politics and religion nor the political radicals nor the devotees of traditional Christianity. These reflections are therefore presented without much hope that they will elicit any general concurrence.[13]

I find myself in substantial agreement with Niebuhr both about the need and about the probable minority appeal of such a position. But orthodoxy has never been the creed of a majority. Nor does the proposal sound very much like an account of Anglicanism. Yet I believe that certain features of the Anglican tradition make the emergence of a traditional and critical orthodoxy possible.

The first feature is the rootedness of much historic and contemporary Anglican existence among grass-roots communities, often among neglected and oppressed communities. In spite of what has been rightly said about the middle-class captivity of Anglicanism, this church has a considerable history of ability to appeal to and have rapport with ordinary people, poor people, insignificant people, and this ability often stands in contrast to the record of political parties, clubs, and trade unions which tend to attract the like-minded and the articulate. A close friend, active in the labour and trade union movements, commented recently that she might start going to church occasionally because

CRITICAL & TRADITIONAL ORTHODOXY

she needed to meet ordinary people. I have emphasised the importance of beginning movements of spiritual renewal and of social justice at the basic neighbourhood level, and there is something very powerful here about the Anglican stress on the parish. Orthodoxy is not a possession but a movement, and it flourishes only when it is shared and lived.

Secondly, there has been an attempt within Anglicanism to hold together a commitment to the historic faith and an openness to new insights. For orthodoxy is not a closed system but a way, a journey. Today there are serious and indeed urgent issues affecting the future shape of orthodoxy. For example, can the tradition of orthodox theology and spirituality incorporate insights from a pluralist society and from the encounter with other faiths? Can the tradition of orthodoxy engage with, and contain, the insights, critiques, and contributions from feminism, and from people of colour? I don't think any of us know the answer to these questions: the jury is still out. But there are elements within the tradition which are hopeful.

Thirdly, there is within the Anglican church a rich tradition of "sacramental materialism." Of course, the rejection of any dualism of matter and spirit, materialism and spirituality, antedates Anglicanism. It has never been more powerfully stated than by St John of Damascus during the iconoclastic controversy of the eighth century.

> I do not worship matter but I worship the Creator of matter who for my sake became material, and accepted to dwell in matter, who through matter effected my salvation. I will not cease from reverencing matter because it was through matter that my salvation came to pass.[14]

But it has been within Anglicanism, and especially within the radical social wing of the Catholic revival, that the unity of sacramental materialism, spirituality, and the demands of justice have received strongest emphasis. At the centre of Anglo-Catholic spirituality is the eucharistic offering. The Anglican refusal to divide worship from action may be one of its most important contributions to the Christian future. As Urban T. Holmes expressed it some years ago:

> We have been asked to choose whether we are interested in prayer or social action, transcendence or immanence, tradition or relevance, orthodoxy or ethicalism, content or process, the Bible or psychology. It is time for the Episcopal Church to refuse to make any such choice, and to live with the apparent contradictions embodied in the acceptance of mutually exclusive categories.[15]

However, I do not think that the resources of this rich and seminal movement of Christian life and experience are easily reclaimable and made available to the people of this age. In order for this to be possible, a great deal of work will be needed. For we are dealing with a confused, demoralised, and polarised community, often polarised on all the wrong issues.

One problem which I have, and which others may share, is that I am not sure where creative and pioneering theological work is currently being done within the framework of the Anglican theological tradition. So I feel rather as Gandhi must have felt when asked for his views on western civilisation. He replied: ''I think it would be a good idea.'' The pursuit of serious theological reflection on these issues within the Anglican framework is a good idea. But how do we move from idea to reality?

I believe that, if we are to make progress in this area, there needs to emerge an Anglican theology of liberation: liberation from the state and from the establishment ethos; liberation from English gentility and from class captivity; liberation from conformity to the dominant culture. The conformity of our churches to mainstream cultural values is a

scandal and a serious disorder with all kinds of conse-
quences. It is, for example, a major element in our failure
to combat racism. For if our general world view on all issues
has come adrift from its biblical and doctrinal roots, it is not
surprising if we fail to resist racism. If we accept the
premises of our society, it is hard to resist its conclusions.
So I believe that the movement towards a subversive
orthodoxy is bound up with the recovery of the theme of
contradiction and of the sense of the church as a counter-
culture. This is a theme which has been recovered and
stressed in the last two decades by some groups and
individuals within the evangelical tradition. Thus Jim Wallis:

> The hope of meaningful countercultural resistance to any
> social or political consensus is not to be found in depreciat-
> ing transcendence or moving in secular directions. That
> practice has in fact become a formula for conformity. On
> the contrary, the church's proper role as an alternative
> corporate reality and prophetic presence in any social
> order will be recovered only as the people of God return
> to their biblical roots and stand firmly on the ground of
> revelation.[16]

Wallis argues that the church needs not only to return to
its theological foundations, its tradition, but also to disaffi-
liate from the dominant culture. This calls for a liberation
of the church and of theology. Such a liberation movement
will be needed if there is to be a renewal of Anglican social
thought, and I believe such a renewal is important and has
significant things to contribute to the changing ecumenical
scene.

A renewed, socially conscious, and critical Anglican tradition could contribute a good deal to the deepening and
strengthening of the spirituality of the future: in relation
to the corporate and prayerful use of the Bible; in relation
to the liturgical renewal; in relation to practical and pastoral

issues; in relation to the character of theology and spirituality; and in many other areas. But, of course, there will have to be a renewal of rigorous intellectual work if this is to happen. I do not know if any of this will happen. The future is open. However, let me conclude by returning briefly to my early experience as a Christian in the 1950s and to the thinking of one important contemporary writer.

The main intellectual influence on my taking the Christian faith seriously in those years was a young philosopher called Alasdair MacIntyre. MacIntyre wrote his first book in 1953 at the age of 24. He began it with some reflections on "The Sacred and the Secular."

> When the sacred and the secular are separated, then ritual becomes an end not to the hallowing of the world but in itself. Likewise if our religion is fundamentally irrelevant to our politics, then we are recognising the political as a realm outside the reign of God. To divide the sacred from the secular is to recognise God's action only within the narrowest limits. A religion which recognises such a division, as does our own, is one on the point of dying.[17]

Almost thirty years later, in 1981, MacIntyre returned, with renewed intensity, to the question of community within the context of moral reasoning. *After Virtue* is a strong attack on liberal individualism, a rootless movement. Modern liberals, MacIntyre claims, have no roots in any living tradition. They speak the languages of everywhere and of nowhere. To MacIntyre, living traditions embody continuities of conflict. The recovery of a living tradition is a major task of our culture as we face a new dark age. For the barbarians are already in our midst, and we are waiting for a new St Benedict.[18] I am not going to enter now into the important debates around that thesis. But I want to go back to the final page of MacIntyre's first book of 1953. Here he sums up what is an urgent necessity today: the rebuilding of Christian communities; the reintegration of politics and prayer; a new eucharistic sensibility arising from, and nourishing, a sacramental materialism; and a solidarity with the marginalised and the outcasts through the recovery of the orthodoxy of one who was poor and incarnate, rejected and slain. This is essentially what I have been trying to say. This is how he ends his book of 1953.

> A community committed alike to politics and to prayer would serve in the renewal of the whole church, for it would give to us a new understanding of the central act of the church's life which is in humble thanksgiving to eat the body of a Lord who hungered and thirsted and to drink the blood of a Lord whom the powers of church and state combined to crucify outside the walls of the city.[19]

References

Chapter One

1 Ruth Glass, letter in *The Times*, 5th August 1967.
2 For a more detailed account of these streets see my essay "A tale of two streets: Cable Street, Brick Lane and organised racism" in Deborah Duncan Honore (ed.), *Trevor Huddleston: essays on his life and work* (Oxford: Oxford University Press, 1988), pp. 53-77.
3 Ashley Smith, *The East Enders* (London: Secker and Warburg, 1961), p. 75.
4 Roi Ottley, *No Green Pastures* (London: John Murray, 1952), p. 29.
5 Patrick O'Donovan, "The challenge of Cable Street", *The Listener*, 16th February 1950, pp. 287-8.
6 Michael Banton, *The Coloured Quarter* (London: Cape, 1955).
7 See Susan J Smith, *The Politics of "Race" and Residence* (Cambridge: Polity Press, 1989).
8 On gentrification see Ruth Glass, *Clichés of Urban Doom and other essays* (Oxford: Blackwell, 1988).
9 A. Sivanandan in *Race and Class*, 23: 2-3 (1981-2), p. 112.
10 Cyril Osborne in *The Guardian*, 27th July 1965.
11 *The Times*, 19th June 1961.

[12] "World in Action", Granada TV, 30th January 1978.

[13] Marion K. Sanders, "The professional radical: conversations with Saul Alinsky", *Harper's Magazine*, June-July 1965.

[14] Conrad Noel, *Jesus the Heretic* (London: Religious Book Club, 1939), p. 27.

[15] Gareth Bennett, *To the Church of England* (Worthing: Churchman Publishing, 1988), pp. 189-228.

[16] *Faith in the City: a call to action by church and nation* (London: Church House Publishing, 1985), pp. xiv, 47, 57, 208, etc.

[17] Richard Gutteridge, *Open Thy Mouth for the Dumb! the German Evangelical Church and the Jews 1879-1950* (Oxford: Blackwell, 1976), p. 191.

[18] Allan A. Boesak, *Comfort and Protest: reflections on the Apocalypse of John of Patmos* (Edinburgh: St Andrew Press, 1987).

[19] John Davies in Kenneth Leech and Rowan Williams, ed., *Essays Catholic and Radical* (London: Bowerdean Press, 1983), p. 188f.

[20] Sharon Welch, *Communities of Resistance and Solidarity* (Maryknoll: Orbis, 1985), p. 74.

Chapter Two

[1] Laurie Taylor in *New Society*, 4th October 1973.

[2] R. D. Laing, *The Politics of Experience and The Bird of Paradise* (Harmondsworth: Penguin, 1971 edn), p. 118.

[3] Kenneth Leech, *Youthquake: the growth of a counter-culture through two decades* (London: Sheldon Press, 1973).

[4] Theodore Roszak, *Unfinished Animal* (London: Faber, 1975), p. 68.

[5] *The Poetical Works of John and Charles Wesley* (London: Wesleyan Methodist Conference Office, 1868), I, xxii.

[6] Donald Dayton, *Theological Roots of Pentecostalism* (Zondervan/Scarecrow Press, 1987).

[7] Richard Holloway, *Tract 1990* (Edinburgh: Diocesan Centre, 1989).
[8] Donald Gray, *Earth and Altar*, Alcuin Club Collections; no. 68 (Norwich: Canterbury Press, 1986).
[9] Stewart Headlam, *The Laws of Eternal Life* (London: Frederick Verinder, 1888), p. 52.
[10] James Adderley, "Christian socialism past and present", *The Commonwealth*, December 1926.
[11] A. M. Ramsey, *From Gore to Temple* (London: Longmans, 1960).
[12] Valerie Pitt in Leech and Williams, p 223.
[13] Jim Wallis, *The Call to Conversion* (Tring: Lion Books, 1982), p. 28; Jose Miguez-Bonino in Rex Ambler and David Haslam, ed., *Agenda for Prophets* (London: Bowerdean Press, 1980), p. 106.
[14] Evelyn Underhill, *An Anthology of the Love of God* (London: Mowbrays, 1953), p. 123f.
[15] Alasdair MacIntyre, *Whose Justice? Which Rationality?* (University of Notre Dame Press and Duckworth, 1988).
[16] Walter Brueggemann, *The Prophetic Imagination* (Philadelphia: Fortress Press, 1978), and many other works.
[17] Gustavo Gutierrez, *A Theology of Liberation* (Maryknoll: Orbis, 1973). For later writing on this theme see Gustavo Gutierrez, *We Drink From Our Own Wells* (London: SCM Press, 1984); Jon Sobrino, *Spirituality of Liberation* (Maryknoll: Orbis, 1988); and other works.
[18] R. H. Tawney, *Commonplace Book* (Cambridge University Press, 1972), p. 51.

Chapter Three

[1] David Nicholls, *Deity and Domination* (London: Routledge, 1989), p. 155.
[2] Augustine, Sermon 256 (PL 38: 1191-3).

[3] Conrad Noel, *Socialism in Church History* (London: Frank Palmer, 1910), p. 96. See also Clive Barrett, *To the Fathers They Shall Go* (London: Jubilee Group, 1984).

[4] William Stringfellow, *Dissenter in a Great Society* (New York: Holt, Rinehart and Winston, 1964).

[5] Maurice Reckitt, *Religion and Social Purpose* (London: SPCK, 1935), p. 12.

[6] Bhikhu Parekh, "Between holy text and moral void", *New Statesman and Society*, 24th March 1989, pp. 29-33.

[7] Fredric Jameson, *Postmodernism or the Cultural Logic of Late Capitalism* (London: Verso, 1991).

[8] Sandra M. Schneiders in Frederic B. Burnham, ed., *Postmodern Theology* (San Francisco: Harper and Row, 1989), pp. 56-73.

[9] R.J. Neuhaus, *The Catholic Moment: the paradox of the church in the postmodern world* (San Francisco: Harper and Row, 1987), p. 151.

[10] Rowan Williams, "What is Catholic orthodoxy?" in Leech and Williams, pp. 11-25.

[11] *Church Times*, 25th September 1987.

[12] E.L. Mascall, *Via Media* (London: Longmans, 1957).

[13] Reinhold Niebuhr, *Reflections on the End of an Era* (New York: Charles Scribners Sons, 1934), pp. ix-x.

[14] John of Damascus, *On Icons* 1: 16.

[15] Urban T. Holmes III in Furman C. Stough and Urban T. Holmes, III, ed., *Realities and Visions. The Church's Mission Today* (New York: Seabury, 1976), p. 183.

[16] Jim Wallis, *Agenda for Biblical People* (New York: Harper and Row, 1976), p. 53.

[17] Alasdair MacIntyre, *Marxism: an interpretation* (London: SCM Press, 1953), pp. 9-10.

[18] Alasdair MacIntyre, *After Virtue* (University of Notre Dame Press and Duckworth, 1981), p. 245.

[19] MacIntyre, *Marxism*, p. 122.

Other Books from ABC Publishing

The Iceberg and the Fire of Love: A Call to Ecological and Social Compassion by Frank Thompson and David Pollock

Vision Quest: Native Spirituality and the Church in Canada by Janet Hodgson and Jayant Kothare

Soft Bodies in a Hard World: Spirituality for the Vulnerable by Charles Davis

From Creation to Resurrection: A Spiritual Journey by Sister Constance Joanna Gefvert, SSJD

The Gift of Courage: Coping with Pain and Suffering by James Wilkes

Anglicanism and the Universal Church: Highways and Hedges 1958–1990 by John Howe with an overview by Colin Craston

Taking Risks and Keeping Faith: Changes in the Church by John Bothwell

Rites for a New Age: Understanding the Book of Alternative Services by Michael Ingham

A Certain Life: Contemporary Meditations on the Way of Christ by Herbert O'Driscoll

Portrait of a Woman: Meditations on the Mother of Our Lord by Herbert O'Driscoll

The Ministry of the Laity: Sharing the Leadership, Sharing the Task by Donald Peel